AF406856

Rachel'sCookbooks© Copyright 2022 - All rights reserved.

Table of Contents

A SPECIAL REQUEST

Your brief amazon review could really help us.

You know, this is very easy to do, go to the ORDERS section of your Amazon account and click on the "Write a review for the product" button. It will automatically take you to the review section.

INTRODUCTION

Christmas is always an extraordinary time, which calls back many memories in my mind.

Memories of when I was a child are often related to food: I couldn't wait for Christmas to come to meet everyone in the family and cook and eat together.

The dishes we prepared for Christmas were all delicious, and helping mum or grandmother prepare them was fun. I was always very excited by the idea of the Christmas atmosphere and the fantastic food cooked.

The intoxicating smell reached up to the dining room.
The funniest part for me was seeing that set of colors and scents directly on the Christmas table.

But on the other hand, food and cooking have always been my passion. That's the reason why I have decided to write this book.

This book brings together all the typical American recipes and all that we prepared at my home or found at the table when I ate with some relatives. These delicious recipes that you will find in this guide will give you different options and will allow you to satisfy even the most demanding palates.

They are also suitable recipes for children.

As I said above, most are part of the traditional American Christmas dinner. When I was a child, my mother always got up early on Christmas morning to bake the turkey that needed many hours of cooking. Even now that I'm an adult, h, turkey, for example, can never miss Christmas Day on our table. Now I just must give you some practical advice on the Christmas table and then show you all the delicious recipes to prepare.

You can opt for both a meat and fish menu or another vegetable option. We just must start!

What do Americans eat on Christmas Day? If you look closely, it recalls a sort of encore of Thanksgiving, the most heartfelt holiday in the United States. Still, some dishes are specific to this period. In any case, the table requires special precautions.

I will give you some useful advice on the traditional table I prepared as a child and still use it today. Having a large family, I have spent many Christmases with the table set and decorated.

Let's start with the color: red is a traditional color and should be used to make the environment warm.

You can choose other colors very well, but tradition cannot be escaped! So, be sure and choose absolutely the red one.

We can choose one of those decorated with a red Christmas theme for the tablecloth.

As for the setting, the same rules of etiquette apply as always: for each place, the plate should be placed in the center, the fork on the left, and the knife on the right with the blade facing inwards.

The spoon also goes to the right and right of the knife, while the spoon or dessert fork goes up horizontally to the plate.

The bread saucer goes up to the left, next to the dessert cutlery. To their right, the glasses go.

Another tip I want to give you is to dedicate a table for children. If there are many guests and many children, why not set up a table for them? I remember when I was little with my little cousins, we always had our table for Christmas or New Year; for us, it was a joy; we felt "great" and could talk freely about our things.

This tradition continues today with my grandchildren, they make noise sitting around their table, and we adults enjoy dinner in peace.

You could adopt the same trick too. You could make an adult table set with fine tablecloths and crockery while the children's table with disposable plates and glasses ... so grandma's dinner service is safe.

In a proper Christmas table, the centerpiece must not be missing; classic or extravagant, it must reflect the host's tastes and the table's setting.
The centerpiece is the heart of the table and the center of attraction for the guests.

It must strike and conquer the guests, but it must not be too bulky; at the table, it is comfortable, and the protagonist must be the food. If we want to use candles as a centerpiece, my advice is not to choose the scented ones ... at the table, the only smell allowed is that of food!

On the market, there are various shapes: low and wide candles are ideal when we want to create a composition, and long and narrow ones to embellish candlesticks.

Another idea for table decoration is that of place markers. We can also indulge our imagination and create them with our hands. Use a sprig of mistletoe, a tiny pinecone, an object made with modeling pastes, a biscuit, or a bar of chocolate. The possibilities are endless!

What we must not forget is a note with the name of our guests.

And if we want to do things big, we can also write the evening menu by hand; I always did it like this: I chose a beautiful parchment, wrote the courses of the evening, and then placed it on the table, so our guests got an idea of all the delights that await them, as if we were at the restaurant.

My advice ends here, even if it seems trivial to say it, the important thing is to spend Christmas lunches and dinners with those who love each other!

Here, put together, are my traditional recipes from the Christmas menu.

Enjoy them!

STARTER RECIPES

These super easy nuggets are perfect for starting the Christmas dinner. Tasty and racy, everyone will like them.

INGREDIENTS

- 8 long jalapeño
- 4 oz of cheddar cheese cut into 8 pieces
- Salt to taste
- 1 tbsp of olive oil

DIRECTIONS

1. First, preheat the oven to 390º F [200º C].
2. Cut off the top of the jalapeno and remove the seeds.
3. Place a piece of cheddar cheese in each jalapeno.
4. Place the jalapeno in the baking pan.
5. Cook jalapeno nuggets for 15-20 minutes circ.
6. Cook until the jalapeno is completely cooked and the cheese is melted.
7. Serve the cheddar and jalapeno nuggets, still hot.

SERVES: 4   **PREP:** 15'   **COOKING:** 15'

A soufflé, which is a very elegant way to start the Christmas meal. This version is really yummy. Everybody will love it!

INGREDIENTS

- 4 eggs
- 1 cup of milk
- ¼ o fall purpose flour
- ½ cup of grated cheddar cheese
- 2 tbsp of chopped onions
- 2 tbsp of butter
- Salt and pepper to taste

DIRECTIONS

1. First, separate the yolks from the whites. Place them in two separate bowls.
2. Beat the egg whites until stiff and set aside.
3. Put the butter in a saucepan and let it melt.
4. Once it is melted, add the all-purpose flour and toast it for a couple of minutes, constantly stirring so as not to burn it.
5. Add the milk a little at a time and keep on stirring.
6. Let the mixture thicken, and then add the Cheddar cheese and shredded onion.
7. Mix until the cheese is completely melted. Turn off the cream.
8. Now, beat the egg yolks and then put them in the mixture with the cheese and onion cream.
9. Stir and when they are completely incorporated, add the egg whites, stirring gently from bottom to top.
10. Brush a soufflé mold with oil and pour the mixture inside.
11. Cook in the hot oven (405°F – 210°C) for 15-20 minutes.
12. Check the cooking of this soufflé; if the mixture has swollen, you can remove them from the oven and serve them immediately inside the same mold.

SERVES: 4   **PREP:** 15'   **COOKING:** 40'

Another very spicy recipe that I may not have loved as a child but which I now include in every Christmas Eve dinner. With these starters, you will be on the safe side.

INGREDIENTS

- 4 large green bell peppers
- 2 tbsp of olive oil
- 1 cup of Monterey Jack cheese, coarsely grated
- 1 shallot, finely chopped
- 2 cloves garlic, finely chopped
- 1/2 red bell pepper, finely chopped
- 2 chili peppers, seeded and chopped
- 1/2 cup chopped fresh parsley
- 1 tsp of powdered ginger
- 1 tbsp of Tabasco sauce
- Salt to taste

DIRECTIONS

1. First, wash green peppers and cut them in half. Then scrape out seeds.
2. Heat two tablespoons of olive oil in a nonstick skillet.
3. Add chopped shallots, garlic, chili, red bell pepper, parsley, and ginger. Cook over medium heat until golden brown for about 4 minutes.
4. Remove pan from heat and stir in hot Tabasco sauce and Monterey cheese.
5. Add a bit of salt and mix.
6. Spoon the mixture into the hollowed bell peppers and sprinkle with the remaining Monterey cheese.
7. Place the bell peppers in a baking pan in the oven at 390ºF [200ºC].
8. Cook until the cheese is browned and the chilies are tender. You will need between 30 to 40 minutes.
9. Remove from the oven and serve your stuffed bell peppers still hot.

SERVES: 4   **PREP:** 5'   **COOKING:** 10'

These fries are perfect as an appetizer! Crunchy and delicious, they will be the ideal start to Christmas dinner or lunch.

INGREDIENTS

- 1 cup of grated cheddar cheese
- ½ tsp of chili powder
- Chopped parsley to taste

DIRECTIONS

1. Start by preheating the oven to 395ºF [200ºC].
2. Line a baking tray with parchment paper and form piles with the cheddar cheese, leaving enough space between one and another.
3. Sprinkle the cheddar cheese with parsley and chili powder.
4. Place the pan in the oven. Cook for 8 minutes, making sure that the cheese does not burn.
5. Let cool, and then serve your cheddar starters.

SERVES: 4   **PREP:** 10'   **COOKING:** 15'

By far my favorite starter as a child. Unable to resist, I ate them very hot, just cooked. On the Christmas table, they represent a decidedly more rustic Christmas dinner.

INGREDIENTS

- 8 large Frankfurters
- 1/3 cup of all-purpose flour
- For the batter
- 2 oz of Corn flour
- 1/3 cup of all-purpose flour
- 1 large Egg
- 2 cups of Whole milk
- 1 tsp of baking soda
- 2 tbsp of Sugar
- 1 pinch of paprika
- 1 pinch of Salt
- For frying
- 5 cups of Seed oil

DIRECTIONS

1. To prepare corn dogs, start by preparing the batter. In a large bowl, pour the corn flour and all-purpose flour. Add the salt and sugar.
2. Then pour in the baking soda and the paprika. Now take a hand whisk and mix the ingredients while gradually adding the milk at room temperature.
3. Add an egg and continue to whisk until the mixture is free of lumps and thick enough. Pour the batter into a cylindrical container with high sides and set aside.
4. At this point, take the frankfurters and cut them in half.
5. Skewer the uncut part of the frankfurters with the skewer.
6. Repeat the operation for all the sausages.
7. Then pass them in the flour, taking care to cover the surface of the sausage entirely, and then dip it into the previously prepared batter.
8. Heat and bring the seed oil to a temperature of 385°F [195°C]; help yourself with a cooking thermometer to reach the exact temperature. Let the excess batter drain slightly and dip them one at a time in the seed oil
9. Fry each piece for about 4 minutes until it is well gold.
10. Place the corn dogs on a sheet of paper towel to remove excess oil, then serve them still hot.

6. CORN BREAD

It's the classic filling used to stuff turkey on Thanksgiving Day. Still, I love consuming the stuffing meat as a delicious Christmas appetizer.

INGREDIENTS

- 1.6 lbs of corn bread
- 1 cup and ½ of cranberries
- 1/4 cup of water
- 1/4 cup of maple syrup
- 2 tbsp of olive oil
- 1 diced onion
- 2 leeks, thinly sliced
- 1 cup of chopped walnuts
- Salt and pepper to taste
- 2 cups of vegetable broth
- 1 tsp of chopped thyme

DIRECTIONS

1. First, cut the corn bread into cubes and leave it to dry at room temperature for at least a day and a night so that it can stay compact and not become too mushy in cooking.
2. Clean and cook the cranberries in the oven with the water and maple syrup at 410ºF [210ºC] for about 15 minutes.
3. In the meantime, brown the onion and leeks in a large pan in the oil with salt and pepper.
4. In a large bowl, pour the diced bread, leeks, onion, walnuts, thyme, vegetable broth, and cranberries. Mix everything very gently.
5. Transfer the mixture to a big baking dish, distributing it evenly, and let it cook (always at 410ºF – 210ºC) for about 30 minutes or until golden brown.
6. Serve your cornbread lukewarm.

7. CRANBERRY SAUCE

We wanted to put it as an appetizer, but this sauce is suitable for practically any dish. Like any self-respecting Christmas menu, the cranberry sauce could not be missing.

INGREDIENTS

- 1 cup and 1/2 of Cranberries
- 1 cup of sugar
- 1/2 cup of Orange Juice
- 1/8 teaspoon of salt
- 1/4 teaspoon of Cinnamon
- 1 tablespoon of Butter
- 1/2 teaspoon of Vanilla

DIRECTIONS

1. To prepare the cranberry sauce, first, wash and let dry cranberries.
2. Put the cranberries in a pan together with the sugar and orange juice.
3. Cook over medium heat, occasionally stirring, until the mixture thickens. Ten minutes in total.
4. When the blueberry sauce has thickened, turn off the heat and add the salt, cinnamon, butter and vanilla, and give one last quick stir.
5. Transfer it to a glass container. Let it rest overnight before serving.

SERVES: 4   **PREP:** 20'   **COOKING:** 50'

I remember this very hot and delicious soup. We used to eat it as a first course during the Christmas holidays, before the turkey! I wanted to propose it again as very tasty, even for the little ones.

INGREDIENTS

- 2 cups of pork loin
- 1 cup of pumpkin pulp
- ½ shallot
- 1 tsp of marjoram
- 1 tsp of chopped basil

- 3/4 cups of water
- salt and pepper to taste
- Olive oil to taste

DIRECTIONS

1. You can start by removing excess of fat, washing, and drying the pork tenderloin. After that operation, cut the pork meat into cubes.
2. Peel and wash the pumpkin, remove all internal seeds, and cut them into cubes.
3. Peel and wash the half shallot and then cut it into thin slices.
4. Wash both marjoram and basil.
5. Heat a bit of olive oil in a saucepan and fry the pumpkin cubes together with shallot slices as soon as it is hot enough.
6. When ten minutes have passed, add the marjoram and basil, mix, and sauté them for a couple of minutes.
7. Now add the pork loin cubes and season everything with salt and pepper. Let sauté for 5 minutes.
8. Add 3 or 4 cups of water and bring the soup to a boil.
9. Keep cooking for 40-45 minutes, then turn it off.
10. Put the pork and pumpkin soup on serving plates, season with a drizzle of oil, and serve immediately.

SERVES: 4   **PREP:** 15'   **COOKING:** 15'

These very easy American muffins will be perfect to start your Christmas dinner or lunch. You can serve it with cranberry sauce. You will love it! Like I have always done.

INGREDIENTS

- 1 egg
- 4 tbsp of all-purpose flour
- 4 cherry tomatoes
- 0.5 tsp of yeast (or baking soda)
- 2 tbsp of grated Parmesan cheese
- ¼ cup of bacon
- Salt and pepper to taste
- Olive oil to taste

DIRECTIONS

1. Wash, dry, and then cut the cherry tomatoes into small pieces.
2. Put the all-purpose flour, yeast, egg, salt, and pepper in a bowl.
3. Stir with a hand whisk, then add a tbsp of olive oil.
4. Mix and add the bacon, cut into small pieces when the dough is homogeneous.
5. Add the cherry tomatoes and grated Parmesan cheese to the bowl with the mixture and mix the mixture thoroughly.
6. Sprinkle a little olive oil in four muffin molds and pour the dough divided into equal parts inside.
7. Cook in the oven at 395°F [200°C] for 10 minutes.
8. Check the cooking and if they are cooked, take them out of the oven. Otherwise, cook for another 2-3 minutes.
9. As soon as they are cooked, take them out of the oven and serve immediately with cranberry sauce.

10. ZUCCHINI AND PECANS CHUNKS

These zucchini and pecans chunks are perfect for starting your Christmas meal. From the largest to the smallest, everyone will love them!

INGREDIENTS

- 1 roll of low-carb shortcrust pastry
- 1 big-sized zucchini
- 12 pecans
- 1 tbsp of Tabasco
- 1 tbsp of Parmesan grated cheese
- ½ cup of half and half
- 4 tbsp of butter

DIRECTIONS

1. First, peel the zucchini, wash it, and cut it into little slices.
2. Rinse zucchini slices under running water and let them dry.
3. Sauté zucchini slices slowly in a pan with a bit of oil, Tabasco, Parmesan cheese, and chopped pecans for half an hour.
4. When the zucchinis are well browned, turn off and pass them in the mixer, leaving them relatively coarse and add the cream to emulsify.
5. It is necessary to obtain a medium consistency, neither liquid nor dry, suitable for filling the dough.
6. After cutting out some dough triangles, fill them with the mixture, close them well and sprinkle with the cream obtained by working the butter.
7. Bake on a baking pan for half an hour at 375ºF [190ºC].
8. Once these chunks are well cooked, serve still hot.

SOUPS

SERVES: 4   **PREP:** 20'   **COOKING:** 1h30'

A super delicious and spicy turkey soup, suitable for a Christmas meal. In addition to being delicious, this soup is sure to keep you warm thanks to its nutritious ingredients.

INGREDIENTS

- 6 oz of turkey breast
- 1 cup of lentils
- 1 small carrot
- 2 tbsp of chopped onions
- 1 tbsp of chopped jalapeno
- 1 sprig of rosemary
- 4/5 cups of vegetable stock
- Salt and pepper to taste
- Olive oil to taste

DIRECTIONS

1. First, heat the vegetable broth.
2. Meanwhile, wash and dry the rosemary.
3. Peel the carrot, jalapeno, and onion. Wash them and then chop them.
4. Rinse the lentils under water and then let them drain.
5. Wash and dry the turkey breast and then cut it in half. Then cut it into cubes.
6. Heat a tablespoon of olive oil in a saucepan. Brown the carrot, onion, jalapeno, and rosemary.
7. After 2 minutes, add the turkey cubes and sauté for 5 minutes.
8. Now add the lentils and mix.
9. Cook for 2-3 minutes and then cover everything with the hot broth. Bring to a boil, season with salt and pepper, and cook for an hour.
10. After the hour, remove the turkey and set it aside. Continue cooking the lentils for another 15 minutes. After 15 minutes, turn off and remove the rosemary.
11. Put the lentils and broth on serving plates.
12. Add the turkey cubes and serve.

SERVES: 4   **PREP:** 20'   **COOKING:** 50'

I remember this hot and delicious soup. We ate it every Sunday! I wanted to propose it to you on your Christmas vacation.

INGREDIENTS

- 16.5 oz of pork loin
- 2 zucchinis
- ½ red onion
- 1 bay leaf
- 3 cups of water

- 1 sprig of rosemary
- 4 bay leaf
- Salt and pepper to taste
- Olive oil to taste

DIRECTIONS

1. Wash and dry the pork tenderloin and cut it into cubes.
2. Peel and wash the zucchini, and then cut them into slices.
3. Peel and wash the red onion and then cut it into thin slices.
4. Wash bay leaves and rosemary.
5. Heat a tablespoon of olive oil in a saucepan and fry the zucchini slices and red onion as soon as it is hot enough.
6. After about ten minutes, add the bay leaf and rosemary, mix, and sauté them for a couple of minutes.
7. Add the pork loin, season with salt and pepper, and sauté for 5 minutes. Add three cups of water and bring to a boil. Continue cooking for 40 minutes, and then turn it off.
8. Put the soup on serving plates, season with a drizzle of oil, and serve immediately.

SERVES: 4   **PREP:** 15'   **COOKING:** 15'

A seafood alternative with this warm ginger-scented shrimp soup.

INGREDIENTS

- 2 cups of shrimps
- 2 cups of vegetable broth
- 1 garlic clove
- 1 tbsp of powdered ginger
- 1 tsp of chopped chives
- Salt and pepper to taste.
- Olive oil

DIRECTIONS

1. First, shell the shrimps, remove the intestinal filament, then wash them and let them drain.
2. Peel the garlic, wash it, and then chop it.
3. Heat a tablespoon of oil in a saucepan and brown the garlic as soon as it is hot.
4. As soon as it is golden brown, add the ginger and broth and bring to a boil.
5. Season with pepper and salt, and then add the shrimps.
6. Continue cooking for 5 minutes and then turn off.
7. Put the soup on plates, sprinkle with chives and serve.

SERVES: 4   **PREP:** 15'   **COOKING:** 30'

I loved sweet potatoes as a child (but I love them even now). Combined with veal, they create a soup that will please everyone.

INGREDIENTS

- 4 slices of lean beef of 4 oz for each
- 1 yellow onion
- 4 sweet potatoes
- 1 tbsp of chopped thyme
- 1 cup of vegetable broth
- All-purpose flour to taste
- Salt and pepper to taste
- Olive oil to taste

DIRECTIONS

1. First, peel the onion and then cut it into thin slices.
2. Peel the sweet potatoes, wash them, and cut them into slices (or little cubes).
3. Wash and dry the thyme, then chop it.
4. Wash and dry the beef slices and then season with salt and pepper.
5. Put the flour on a plate and then flour the slices and set aside.
6. Heat a tablespoon of oil in a pan and brown the onion for a couple of minutes.
7. Now put the sweet potatoes and cook them for 10 minutes.
8. Season with salt and pepper, and put the meat. Brown the meat for 4 minutes per side.
9. Add the broth and thyme and cook for another 15-20 minutes.
10. Put the soup on serving plates and serve.

SERVES: 4   **PREP:** 15'   **COOKING:** 45'

This fragrant soup creates a great Christmas atmosphere. You can also use hot and super delicious as a first course.

INGREDIENTS

- 2 cups and 1/2 of beef pulp
- 1 tomato
- 1 tsp of cardamom
- 2 tbsp of chopped onion.
- 1 sprig of chopped parsley
- 1.1. lbs of water
- 1 sprig of chopped coriander
- Olive oil to taste
- Salt and pepper to taste.

DIRECTIONS

1. Wash and dry the beef and then cut it into cubes.
2. Wash the tomato and then cut it into cubes.
3. Peel and wash the onion and then chop it.
4. Put a tablespoon of olive oil in a saucepan and brown the onion as soon as it is hot.
5. Add tomato, parsley, and coriander when the onion is golden brown.
6. Stir, cook for a couple of minutes and then add the beef cubes.
7. Cook beef cubes for 5 minutes, then add salt, pepper, and cardamom.
8. Stir, cook well, and then add 1.1. lbs of water. Bring to a boil, and then continue cooking for another 15 minutes.
9. As soon as the soup is cooked, turn it off and transfer it to serving dishes. Season with oil and a sprinkle of black pepper, and serve.

MEAT FIRST DISHES

SERVES: 4   **PREP:** 15'   **COOKING:** 20'

It could not be missing from our Christmas menu, one of the most loved dishes by Americans. With the famous Alfredo sauce, I ate at least one whole dish.

INGREDIENTS

- 2 cups of fettuccine
- 1 cup of chicken breast
- ¼ cup of butter
- 1 cup of cooking cream (or half and half)
- ½ cup of grated Parmesan cheese
- 1 pinch of grated nutmeg
- salt
- pepper

DIRECTIONS

1. First, clean and wash the chicken breast.
2. Cut the chicken into strips. Cook it with salt, pepper and half the butter in a non-stick pan, browning it well.
3. Set the chicken aside and season the cream with salt, pepper, nutmeg and the remaining butter in the same pan. Then add the chicken again.
4. Meanwhile, cook the pasta, drain it "al dente" and then toss it in the pan with the sauce, stirring with the Parmesan cheese.
5. The fettuccine Alfredo with chicken is ready. You just have to taste them.

17. BAKED ZITI

SERVES: 4 **PREP:** 15' **COOKING:** 90'

This great classic from the United States that can also be served at Christmas. Very tasty, children will especially like it.

INGREDIENTS

- 30.5 oz of pasta ziti
- 4 cups of Italian sausage
- 1 jar of spaghetti sauce
- 1 jar of Alfredo sauce
- 1 cup of divided mozzarella
- ½ cup of grated provolone

- 1/3 cup of grated Parmesan cheese divided
- ½ cup of panko breadcrumbs
- 1½ teaspoon of chopped garlic in a jar
- 2 tablespoons of olive oil
- salt and pepper to taste

DIRECTIONS

1. Preheat the oven to 350ºF [175ºC] degrees. Spray a 9 × 13-inch [20x30 cm] baking dish with cooking spray. To put aside.
2. Cook the pasta according to the package directions. Drain and set aside.
3. In a large skillet, cook the sausage until it is no longer pink. Drain the fat.
4. Add the spaghetti sauce, the Alfredo sauce, 1/2 of mozzarella, provolone, and 1/2 of Parmesan. Boil until the cheeses melt.
5. Mix the cooked pasta and pour it into the prepared pan. Top with the remaining mozzarella.
6. Combine the remaining Parmesan cheese, panko breadcrumbs, garlic, and olive oil. Sprinkle with the pasta.
7. Cook uncovered for 35 minutes until bubbly, and the topping turns golden brown.
8. Serve baked ziti still hot.

18. PEA, CHERRY TOMATOES, AND BACON SOUP

This homemade-flavored soup is an excellent choice for those who want to make the first course but is still very good.

INGREDIENTS

- 1 cup of cubed smoked bacon
- 1 cup of frozen peas
- 8 cherry tomatoes
- 2 spring onions
- 3 cups of meat stock

- 1 chili
- Olive oil to taste
- Salt and pepper to taste

DIRECTIONS

1. Wash and dry the cherry tomatoes and cut them into cubes. Cube smoked bacon too.
2. Wash and dry the spring onions and cut them into thin slices.
3. Wash and dry the chili and then cut it into small pieces.
4. Put a drizzle of olive oil in a large pot.
5. Sauté the spring onions for a minute, and then add the tomatoes and peas.
6. Stir and season with pepper and salt. Cook for a couple of minutes, and then add the cubed bacon and chili. Mix and season, and then cover everything with the fish broth.
7. Cook for 15 minutes, adjust, if necessary, with salt and pepper and then turn off.
8. Put the hot soup on serving plates and serve.

SERVES: 4 **PREP:** 5' **COOKING:** 10'

A simple dish will help if you have little time to prepare a Christmas first course. The sausage makes this dish unique in flavor.

INGREDIENTS

- 1 cup of sausage
- 2 cups of baby spinach
- 2 tbsp of chopped onion
- 1 cup of vegetable broth

- Salt and pepper to taste
- olive oil to taste

DIRECTIONS

1. Clean the spinach, then wash and dry them.
2. Put the broth in a saucepan and bring it to a boil.
3. Add the spinach, season with salt and pepper, and mix.
4. Cook for 7 minutes and then turn off. With an immersion blender, blend everything until you get a homogeneous mixture.
5. Meanwhile, cook the chopped sausage in a pan with the chopped onion.
6. Brown everything well for about ten minutes.
7. Put the cream of spinach on serving plates and put them on top of the sausage with the onion.
8. Season with a drizzle of raw oil and serve.

20. TURKEY PORK AND PEPPERS RICE

I often ate this dish as a guest with my uncles on Christmas day. Made with pork and turkey, it's a tasty dish that I'm sure you'll like too.

INGREDIENTS

- 14 oz of rice
- 1 cup of turkey breast
- ½ cup of pork loin
- Half onion
- 1 small red pepper
- 3 cups of vegetable broth
- 1 tsp of cardamom powder
- 1 tsp of turmeric
- 1 tsp of chopped chives
- Salt and pepper to taste
- Olive oil to taste

DIRECTIONS

1. Bring the vegetable broth to a boil and cook the black rice for 25 minutes.
2. Meanwhile, wash the turkey and pork loin, pat them dry with a paper towel and then cut it into cubes.
3. Remove the cap, the seeds, and the white filaments of the pepper. Wash it and cut it into cubes.
4. Peel the onion, wash it, and then chop it.
5. Heat a tablespoon of olive oil in a pan and put the onion to brown as soon as it is hot.
6. Add the pepper, stir, and cook for 5 minutes.
7. Add the cardamom, turmeric and a glass of water, and cook for another 2 minutes.
8. Add the turkey and pork, season with salt and pepper, and cook for 10 minutes. When the meat is cooked, turn it off and set it aside.
9. At this point, the cooking of the rice will be completed. Drain it and place it in the pan with the turkey and pork.
10. Stir to mix well, and then transfer the rice to serving plates. Sprinkle with chives and serve.

FISH FIRST DISHES

SERVES: 4   **PREP:** 15'   **COOKING:** 90'

Clam chowder is a famous American soup made with clams, potatoes, bacon, and cream to be eaten with croutons or in a loaf. I loved eating it, even at Christmas.

INGREDIENTS

- 3 lbs of Clams
- 1.5 lbs of Potatoes
- ½ cup of Bacon
- 1 shallot
- 1 cup of cooking cream
- 3 tbsp of Butter
- Vegetable broth as required
- Salt and pepper to taste

DIRECTIONS

1. First, drain the fresh clams in cold and salted water for about two hours to eliminate all impurities and sand.
2. Once clean, take the clams and put them open on the fire in a pot with a closed lid for a couple of minutes.
3. When all the clams have opened, shell them and set them aside, then strain the broth that has formed in the pot and add it to the hot vegetable broth.
4. Wash and peel the potatoes, cut them into small cubes, and finely chop the onion. Also, cut the bacon into cubes.
5. Melt the butter in a saucepan. Then add the shallot, and brown it slightly; add the bacon and sauté for a few minutes.
6. Add the potatoes and start cooking them, gradually adding the hot broth.
7. When the potatoes are cooked, take about half of them and blend them; add them back to the pot and add the cream.
8. Mix the soup well, and season with salt and pepper. Lastly, add the shelled clams.
9. Serve hot with croutons or a loaf.

SERVES: 4   PREP: 15'   COOKING: 90'

It's a typical delicious Creole dish from New Orleans. We often did it at Christmas, and I was always very greedy.

INGREDIENTS

- 1.1. lbs of Basmati-type rice
- 3 cups of Shrimps
- 2 cups of Tomato pulp
- ½ cup of Chorizo
- 2 Green peppers
- 1 Onion
- 4 tbsp of Celery
- 2 tbsp of olive oil
- 2 tbsp of Cajun spice mix
- Parsley to taste
- Black pepper to taste
- For the chicken broth:
- 2.5 lbs of Chicken drumsticks
- 4 lbs of Water
- ½ cup of Carrots
- ½ cup Onions
- 2 tbsp Celery
- 2 tbsp of Coarse salt
- 2 tbsp of Jamaican pepper in grains

DIRECTIONS

1. To make the jambalaya, prepare the chicken broth: peel and coarsely chop the onion, celery, and carrots, then remove the skin from the chicken drumsticks with the help of a knife.

2. Pour the vegetables and chicken into a large pot, add the coarse salt and the Jamaican peppercorns, then cover everything with water.

3. Cook the broth for 50 minutes from the moment the water reaches a boil. After this time, filter the broth and keep it warm to one side, then strip the chicken, separating the meat from the bones and nerves.

4. Now you can move on to the preparation of the jambalaya: peel and cut into small cubes the green peppers 10, the onion, and

the celery.

5. Heat the oil in a saucepan, add
    the vegetables and fry over
    medium heat for about 10 minutes.
    In the meantime, also cut the
    chorizo into cubes.

6. After 10 minutes, add the chorizo
    to the sauté, chicken meat, and
    Cajun spice mix. Stir well and cook
    over medium heat for another 10
    minutes.

7. Add the rice and toast it for a
    minute, then pour the chicken
    broth until it is abundantly
    covered.

8. 8.   Add the tomato sauce, cover
    with the lid, and cook for about 18
    minutes (or for the time indicated
    on the rice package). Check from
    time to time that the liquid has not
    dried too much.

9. After 10 minutes, add the whole
    shrimps, close with the lid, and
    continue cooking.

10. After the cooking time of the rice,
    the jambalaya must still be slightly
    soupy on the bottom.

11. Turn off the heat, add freshly
    ground black pepper and some
    fresh chopped parsley, and your
    jambalaya is ready to be enjoyed.

Merry Christmas

23. MUSSEL AND MINT CREAMY SOUP

SERVES: 4   PREP: 20'   COOKING: 15'

This delicious mint-flavored soup was one of our fish alternatives when we decided to propose a natural menu a little different than usual.

INGREDIENTS

- 2.2. lbs of mussels
- 1 shallot
- 1 cup of half and half
- 1 tbsp of chopped mint
- 1 glass of brandy
- Salt and pepper to taste
- Olive oil to taste

DIRECTIONS

1. First, peel and wash the shallot and cut it into thin slices.
2. Scrape the shell of the mussels, remove the external beard, and then wash them thoroughly under running water.
3. Wash and dry the mint.
4. Put the mussels brandy and mint in a pan, cover them with a lid and let them open.
5. Once opened, remove them from the pan and remove the shell that does not contain the mollusk. Strain the cooking juices into another bowl.
6. Put a tablespoon of olive oil in a saucepan and let it heat up.
7. When hot, sauté the shallot for a couple of minutes.
8. Now add the cooking juices and half and half and mix well.
9. Cook for 5 minutes, and then add the mussels.
10. Cook for 2 minutes, season with salt and pepper and then turn off.
11. Put the soup on serving plates, sprinkle with chopped parsley and serve.

SERVES: 4   **PREP:** 20'   **COOKING:** 40'

I often eat this rice during the winter, but it has something extraordinary at Christmas. This is the ideal first course if you decide to make a fish menu.

INGREDIENTS

- 2 cups of rice
- 2 cups of pumpkin pulp
- 20 king prawns
- 1 onion

- 3 cups of vegetable broth
- 1 sage leaves
- Salt and pepper to taste
- Olive oil to taste

DIRECTIONS

1. Wash and dry the pumpkin pulp, remove seeds and filaments if present, and cut it into cubes.
2. Shell the king prawns, remove the intestinal filament, wash them, and pat them with absorbent paper.
3. Peel and wash the onion, then chop it.
4. Wash and dry the sage.
5. Heat a tablespoon of olive oil in a pan.
6. As soon as it is hot, sauté the onion and sage.
7. After 2 minutes, add the pumpkin and prawns.
8. Sauté for 5 minutes, and then add the rice.
9. Toast for 2 minutes, and then start adding a ladle of broth.
10. Stir and let all the broth absorb before adding the other.
11. Repeat the same operation until the end of the broth.
12. As soon as you have finished cooking, put the prawns and pumpkin on serving plates, season with a drizzle of oil, and serve.

This very spicy cream is for the most demanding palates. Offer it as a first fish dish instead of some spiced meat soup.

INGREDIENTS

- 1 broccoli
- 3 tbsp of chopped onion
- 2 cups of hot vegetable broth
- 1 tbsp of chopped jalapeno
- 1 cup of smoked salmon

- 1 sprig of dill
- 2 tbsp of olive oil
- Salt and pepper to taste

DIRECTIONS

1. First, wash the broccoli thoroughly under running water. Dry it and then cut it into small pieces.
2. Peel the onion and jalapeno (removing all seeds), then wash dry and chop finely.
3. Take a large pan and heat the olive oil. As soon as it is hot, put the onion and jalapeno to brown.
4. After 1 minute, add the broccoli.
5. Sauté for a couple of minutes, seasoning with salt and pepper.
6. Add the vegetable broth and cook with a lid for another 25 minutes.
7. Check the cauliflower and cook for another 5 minutes if it is still not soft enough.
8. Once cooked, put the broccoli in the blender's glass, and blend until you get a smooth and creamy mixture. Put the soup on the plate. Dress it in a velvety sauce with the rolled salmon slices.
9. Sprinkle with dill and serve.

MAIN COURSE MEAT RECIPES

SERVES: 4   PREP: 15'   COOKING: 30'

This pork and bacon recipe is another main course of meat that cannot be missing from the Christmas menu. Succulent and tasty, it will appeal to everyone, from the oldest to the youngest.

INGREDIENTS

- 14 oz of pork loin
- 2 shallots
- 2 tbsp of chopped bacon
- ¼ cup of apple cider vinegar
- 1 green apple
- 2 tbsp of all-purpose flour
- 2 tbsp of mustard
- salt and pepper to taste
- olive oil to taste

DIRECTIONS

1. Start by removing fat and skin from the pork loin. Now wash it and dry it. Cut the pork loin in half by making an incision on one side of the meat at half height.
2. Sprinkle the meat with pepper and salt, then set aside.
3. Peel and wash the shallots and then chop them.
4. Wash the green apple, remove the central core and seeds, and cut them into cubes.
5. Heat a tablespoon of oil in a pan. Add the apples and season with pepper and salt as soon as it is hot. Stir, and cook for 5 minutes. Put the apples in a bowl and let them cool.
6. Add the bacon, flour, and chopped shallots to the bowl with the apples.
7. Combine all ingredients to obtain a homogeneous mixture.
8. Take the pork loin and stuff it along the entire surface. Roll up the meat on itself and seal the meat with kitchen twine.
9. Now put the vinegar, mustard, and two tablespoons of oil in a bowl and mix.

10. Brush the meat with the mustard emulsion.

11. Preheat the oven to 395ºF [200ºC]. Place the pork in a baking pan. Let cook in the oven for 25-30 minutes.

12. Brush from time to time with the mustard emulsion.

13. When pork loin is cooked, let it rest for 15 minutes, cut it into slices, and serve with apple and bacon.

SERVES: 4   **PREP:** 10'   **COOKING:** 20'

Roast beef is a traditional American recipe. Our version was the one with carrots and pecans. So delicious!!

INGREDIENTS

- 4 slices of roast beef of 5 oz for each
- 1 cup of chopped carrots
- 1 white onion
- 4 tbsp of chopped pecans
- Salt and pepper to taste
- Olive oil to taste

DIRECTIONS

1. First, wash and pat the beef meat with a paper kitchen towel, then cut it into strips.
2. Peel and wash the onion and then chop it.
3. Peel, wash, and dry the carrot and chop as well.
4. Put a tablespoon of olive oil in a pan, and then add the chopped onion.
5. Brown it for a couple of minutes, and then add the beef.
6. Sauté for 4-5 minutes, season with salt and pepper, then remove and set aside.
7. Now put the carrot in the same pan.
8. Cook for 13-15 minutes, then season with salt and pepper.
9. Meanwhile, chop the pecans.
10. As soon as the beef has finished cooking, turn it off and distribute it on plates, along with the carrots.
11. Sprinkle the meat with the chopped pecans and serve.

SERVES: 4   **PREP:** 10'   **COOKING:** 210'

Another classic Christmas meat, or the roast goose. Accompanied by carrots and very tender, I couldn't wait for Christmas to finally eat it.

INGREDIENTS

- 2.2 lbs of Goose
- 3 tbsp of Butter
- 1 Carrot
- 1 Red onion
- 1 celery coast
- 1 tbsp of all-purpose flour

- 1 glass of red wine
- 2 cups of Vegetable stock
- 6 tbsp extra virgin olive oil
- Salt and Pepper to taste

DIRECTIONS

1. Wash the goose already clean and dry with a paper towel. Set aside.
2. Peel, wash, and chop both onion and carrot.
3. Clean and chop celery as well.
4. Salt and pepper the goose externally and internally, and put it in a large pan. Sprinkle it with extra virgin olive oil, add the chopped onion, the chopped carrot and the chopped celery, and mix well.
5. Brown the goose well in all its parts over moderate heat for 10 minutes.
6. Transfer the browned goose with all its seasoning to a baking sheet and cover it with aluminum foil for food.
7. Bake in a hot oven at 390°F [200°C] for 210 minutes. During cooking, now and then, prick the goose with a fork to let it is fat out.
8. Remove the goose from the oven and drain it onto the baking tray, place it on a serving plate and keep warm.
9. Transfer the cooking juices to a non-stick pan, also detaching the sauce still attached to the pan.

10. Put the pan on moderate heat,
    pour the red wine, and let it
    evaporate a little. Add 1 ladle of
    vegetable broth and cook for 5
    minutes, stirring constantly.

11. Pass the sauce through a sieve
    on a non-stick pan, add the butter
    and flour, and continue mixing
    until the consistency of a sauce is
    obtained. Then remove from heat
    and pour into a gravy boat.

12. Serve your goose with the sauce
    on the table on a serving plate or
    divide it into pieces and serve to
    each diner on an individual plate
    with the gravy boat available.

This first version of the turkey is made with garlic and butter. I remember the tenderness of turkey meat accompanied by baked potatoes. They are ideal for this recipe.1 kg turkey breast.

INGREDIENTS

- 1 glass of white wine
- 2.2. lbs of turkey breast
- ¼ cup of butter
- 1 garlic clove
- 1 tsp of chopped rosemary
- 1 tsp of chopped sage
- salt to taste
- olive oil to taste

DIRECTIONS

1. Buy a piece of turkey breast and have the butcher tie it if you can't do it.
2. Oil the piece of turkey meat and salt it lightly by massaging.
3. Take a pot or saucepan, put 4 tablespoons of oil and the butter, and let them heat.
4. Put the rosemary and sage in the pot with a clove of garlic and cook for a few minutes.
5. Cook the piece of turkey breast meat over high heat, browning it on all sides to seal the meat.
6. When you have browned all sides of the meat, add the white wine, and let it evaporate.
7. When the wine has completely evaporated, decide if you want to finish cooking it in a pot or the oven.
8. After browning in the pot, transfer the roast turkey to an ovenproof dish and sprinkle it with the sauce from the pot.
9. Cover with silver paper or parchment paper and cook in a preheated oven at 405°F for about 40 minutes. Then remove the paper, wet it with its sauce, and continue cooking, turning it a couple of times for another 10 minutes.
10. Remove the roast turkey from the oven and wrap it silver paper.
11. Wait 9-10 minutes before slicing it and serving it with its sauce.

MAIN COURSE FISH RECIPES

SERVES: 4   PREP: 10'   COOKING: 20'

It's my mother's favorite recipe. We used to cook it at Christmas time. A second meat dish that will conquer everyone … especially Turkey lovers.

INGREDIENTS

- 4 turkey slices (1 cup about for each)
- 2 cups of zucchini
- 2 cups of mushrooms
- 1 chopped garlic clove
- 1/2 cup of lime juice
- 1 tbsp of chopped mint
- Salt and pepper to taste

DIRECTIONS

1. First, you can preheat the oven to 405°F [210°C].
2. Continue to prepare this recipe by washing the zucchini.
3. Clean the mushrooms with a clean cloth and remove any soil. If necessary, wash them under running water.
4. Cut the zucchini into thin slices and the mushrooms into pieces.
5. Peel and chop the garlic clove as well.
6. Spread some baking paper on a baking pan.
7. Place the chopped garlic, mushroom, and zucchini in the center of the pan sheet.
8. Place the turkey slices on the side and season with salt and pepper.
9. Squeeze ½ cup of lime juice over it.
10. Add the chopped mint.
11. Now, you can close the parchment paper creating a sort of foil.
12. Cook the turkey in a preheated oven for about 15-20 minutes.
13. Always check the cooking of the turkey, zucchini, and mushrooms.
14. Serve this recipe lukewarm.

This very light dish will surely help you to arrive at the dessert less weighted. I love cod, but you can use any other type of fish.

INGREDIENTS

- 2 cod fillets of 14 oz for each
- 2 tsp of spicy paprika
- 1 tbsp of Tabasco sauce
- The grated rind of a lime
- Olive oil to taste
- Salt and pepper to taste

DIRECTIONS

1. Wash and dry the cod fillets and remove all the bones present.
2. Brush a pan with olive oil and place the cod fillets inside, with the skin side facing down.
3. Season with oil and then sprinkle with salt, Tabasco sauce, pepper, and paprika.
4. Put the pan in the oven and cook at 395ºF [200ºC] for 15 minutes.
5. When the cod is cooked, remove it from the oven and let it rest for 5 minutes.
6. Now put it on serving plates, sprinkle with lime zest and serve.

SERVES: 6   PREP: 10'   COOKING: 15'

A delicious scallops dish, suitable for Christmas: anyone will love it !!!

INGREDIENTS

- 20 scallops
- 1 cup panko
- 4 tbsp of chopped pecans
- 2 tbsp of grated Parmesan cheese
- 1 tbsp of chopped parsley

- 1 lemon zest
- Salt and pepper to taste
- Olive oil to taste

DIRECTIONS

1. Start this recipe by cleaning the scallops. Rinse them under water, then put them in a bowl with water and coarse salt for about 25-30 minutes.
2. After that, open the shells in two with a small knife, cutting the muscle of the scallop.
3. Now, you should remove the fruit from the shell. Also remove the transparent and the dark parts.
4. Leave the fish to drain in a colander and put the shell where the fruit was attached to one side.
5. Prepare the breading. Mix the panko, chopped parsley, pecans, and grated Parmesan in a bowl. Add 4 tbsp of olive oil and 4 tbsp of water to the mixture.
6. Place the scallop shells directly in an oiled baking pan.
7. Insert the scallop into the shell and cover everything with the panko and pecans mixture for the filling.
8. Sprinkle the surface of the scallops with a bit of olive oil.
9. Preheat the oven to 390°F [200°C]. Cook the scallops for about 10 minutes.
10. Check if they are cooked and serve still hot with lime zest.

SERVES: 4   **PREP:** 20'   **COOKING:** 8'

A salmon dish with an exotic taste, which will please everyone. Very fast, because it is prepared in the microwave, it will allow you to remedy if you need to prepare a quick fish dish.

INGREDIENTS

- 2 salmon filets of 10.5 oz about for each
- 2 cups of pineapple pulp
- 2 tbsp of olive oil
- Salt and pepper to taste
- 1 tsp of parsley
- 1 tbsp of chopped jalapeno

DIRECTIONS

1. First, rinse the filets of salmon under running water.
2. After washing them, drain and dry them with a kitchen paper towel.
3. Flavor the fish with salt and pepper.
4. Add the washed parsley.
5. Meanwhile, peel and take the pulp from the pineapple.
6. Wash pineapple pulp and cut it into cubes.
7. Cook the salmon at maximum power (800 watts) for 3/4 minutes.
8. When cooking has arrived at 2 minutes, add pineapple cubes.
9. If you are not satisfied with the cooking, cook for another minute.
10. Decorate with parsley and chopped jalapeno, and serve.

SERVES: 4   **PREP:** 15'   **COOKING:** 15'

A baked cod dish with a delicious crust. We always prepare it at Christmas as an alternative to meat.

INGREDIENTS

- 3 cups of cod already soaked and desalted
- 3 tbsp of toasted and chopped pine nuts
- 12 cherry tomatoes
- ½ shallot
- 1 tbsp of dried rosemary
- ½ lime
- 1 tsp of chopped coriander
- Olive oil to taste
- Salt and Pepper To Taste.

DIRECTIONS

1. First, wash and dry the already soaked and desalted cod, then pat it dry with a kitchen paper towel.
2. Brush a pan with olive oil and then put the cod inside.
3. Peel and wash the half shallot and then chop it.
4. Wash and dry the lime and then finely grate the zest
5. Wash and dry the cherry tomatoes and then cut them into small cubes.
6. Wash and dry the coriander and then chop it.
7. Sprinkle the cod with chopped tomatoes, pine nuts, shallots, lime zest, and coriander.
8. Sprinkle with chopped rosemary and place the pan in the oven.
9. Cook at 405°F for about 15 minutes.
10. Once cooked, remove the pan from the oven and let the breaded cod rest for a couple of minutes.
11. Put the cod in the serving dishes and serve.

SERVES: 4   PREP: 10'   COOKING: 20'

A second fish dish that will conquer every tuna lover.

INGREDIENTS

- 4 tuna fillets (7 oz about for each)
- 2 medium size zucchinis
- 1 cup of mushrooms
- 1 shallot
- ½ orange
- 1 tbsp of chopped parsley
- Salt and pepper to taste

DIRECTIONS

1. First, preheat the oven to 405ºF [210ºC].
2. Clean the tuna fillet under running water and dry it, and in the meantime, wash the zucchini.
3. Clean the mushrooms with a cloth, removing any soil.
4. Cut the mushrooms into 4 pieces and the zucchini into slices.
5. Peel and chop the shallot too.
6. Spread some baking paper on a baking sheet.
7. Place the shallot, mushroom, and zucchini in the pan.
8. Place the tuna fillet.
9. Season fillets with salt and pepper.
10. Squeeze the orange over it add the chopped parsley.
11. Close the parchment paper creating a sort of foil.
12. Cook the tuna in a preheated oven for about 20 minutes.
13. Always check the cooking of the tuna, zucchini, and mushrooms.
14. You can serve when the tuna and vegetables are cooked.

VEGETABLE MAIN COURSE

36. BOSTON BAKED BEANS

SERVES: 4   **PREP:** 15'   **COOKING:** 6h

Boston baked beans in bean pot is an American recipe that can be perfectly prepared even at Christmas. To be enjoyed instead of meat and fish, it will suit everyone. However, this recipe must be prepared in advance.

INGREDIENTS

- 3 cups of Cannellini beans
- 1 tsp of baking soda
- 1 cup of Bacon
- 1 White onion
- 4 tbsp of Sugar
- 1 glass of Molasses
- 1 tbsp of Mustard
- 1 tbsp of Salt
- 1 tbsp of Pepper

DIRECTIONS

1. Soak the beans the night before.
2. In the morning, preheat the oven to 350ºF [175ºC].
3. Fill half of a pressure cooker with water and add the baking soda.
4. Boil the water, and then add the beans.
5. Cook for about ten minutes, then drain the beans and set them aside.
6. Cut the bacon into cubes. Put half of it in the bottom of the saucepan together with the chopped onion.
7. Add the beans and the rest of the bacon cubes.
8. Prepare a mixture of sugar, molasses, mustard, salt, and pepper with three glasses of hot water, which you will then add to the beans.
9. Cover the saucepan and put it in the oven.
10. Cook for 6 hours, periodically checking the humidity level and adding more water if necessary.
11. Remove the saucepan from the oven and serve.

It's an excellent alternative for those who do not want to eat Christmas meat and fish.

INGREDIENTS

- 2 eggplants
- 1 cup of diced cheddar
- 1 cup of tomato puree
- Salt and pepper to taste
- Olive oil to taste
- Dried oregano to taste
- A few basils leaves to decorate

DIRECTIONS

1. Wash the eggplants, cut them into slices, and drain them in a salt-colored colander.
2. Brush a baking tray with olive oil.
3. Put the eggplant slices inside, and season them with a drizzle of oil and pepper.
4. Bake the eggplant slices in the oven at 405ºF [210ºC] for 20 minutes.
5. After 20 minutes, remove the pan from the oven and place it on a surface.
6. Sprinkle the surface of the eggplants with the tomato puree, and then put a few cheddars on each slice.
7. Sprinkle with oregano. Put back in the oven to cook for another 5 minutes.
8. As soon as they are cooked, remove them from the oven, place them in serving dishes and serve decorated with basil leaves.

SERVES: 4   PREP: 30'   COOKING: 15'

I loved these croquettes at Christmas dinners or lunches. But children love them even now! Success is guaranteed.

INGREDIENTS

- 3 medium potatoes
- 1 tbsp of milk
- 1 cup of all-purpose flour
- 2 tbsp of grated Parmesan cheese
- 1 tbsp of chopped nuts
- ½ cup of panko
- 2 tsp of finely chopped parsley
- leaves
- 1 pinch of paprika
- Olive oil to taste
- Salt and pepper to taste

DIRECTIONS

1. First, wash and peel the 3 potatoes, then cut them into cubes.
2. Wash the parsley and chop it finely.
3. After this operation, boil the potato cubes in salted water for 15 minutes.
4. Once cooked, drain and mash them finely in a large bowl using a potato masher or ricer. Let cool potatoes completely.
5. Mix in the milk, parmesan cheese, all-purpose flour, and parsley. Season with salt, pepper, and paprika.
6. With the potato filling, shape into the size of little golf balls and set aside.
7. Preheat at the same time, the oven to 375ºF [190ºC].
8. Mix the nuts and panko and stir until the mixture becomes loose and crumbly.
9. Place each potato ball into the all-purpose flour, then the panko and roll into a croquette shape.
10. Press coating to croquettes to ensure it adheres to the panko.
11. Place the potato croquettes into the baking pan, then put it in the oven at 375ºF [190ºC]. Let the croquettes cook for 20/22 minutes or until they become golden brown.
12. Serve hot with your favorite sauce.

A gratin that we prepared at Christmas, with this typical Californian cheese. Tasty, everyone will like it and will make you look good with your guests.

INGREDIENTS

- 5 sweet potatoes
- ½ cup of Humboldt Fog (cubed)
- 2 tbsp of grated Parmesan cheese
- ½ cup of milk
- ½ cup half and half
- pinch of paprika
- pinch of cinnamon

DIRECTIONS

1. First, preheat your oven to 405ºF [210ºC].
2. Meanwhile, wash, peel and slice the sweet potatoes thin.
3. In a bowl, mix the milk and half and half and season to taste with salt, pepper, cinnamon, and paprika.
4. Add Humboldt Fog cut into little cubes.
5. Coat the sweet potato slices with the milk mixture.
6. Transfer the sweet potato slices into a baking pan. Pour the rest of the half and half mixture from the bowl on top of the potatoes.
7. Place the baking pan in the oven.
8. Close the lid: Let cook for about 15-20 minutes.
9. After 10 minutes, pour Parmesan cheese evenly over sweet potatoes.
10. Cook until your sweet potatoes' gratin is browned and the Humboldt fog is melted.
11. Serve this delicious gratin still hot.

40. VEGGIES TACOS

A completely vegetarian version of the classic tacos. To be enjoyed by everyone isn't a meat or fish lover.

INGREDIENTS

- 4 crunchy tacos
- 1 minced zucchini
- 1 cup of peppers
- ¼ cup of onion
- 1 tsp of smoked paprika
- 1 tbsp of olive oil
- Salt to taste
- Pepper as needed
- Water if necessary
- Taco Salsa

DIRECTIONS

1. Wash the peppers, dry them, and cut them into strips that are not too long after removing the seeds and the inner white part.
2. Peel, wash, and minced zucchini.
3. In a non-stick pan, start heating three tablespoons of extra virgin olive oil. Add the finely chopped onion and let it brown for about two minutes over medium heat.
4. Withered onions, add and sauté the peppers in a pan for 5 minutes over medium heat. When the oil begins to dry, dilute the mixture with a spoon of water and let it cook for another 10 minutes.
5. Ready the peppers, insert the minced zucchini and let it brown for 10 minutes.
6. Add salt, pepper and paprika, and the filling for your tacos is ready.
7. Fill your tacos with a veil of Taco Salsa and serve.

SIDE DISHES

FOR 25 BISCUITS   **PREP:** 15'   **COOKING:** 35'

Mashed potatoes are a classic recipe for our Christmas. This recipe is very creamy and tasty to accompany the turkey. They are also perfect as a side dish for any recipe.

INGREDIENTS

- 4 cups of potatoes (yellow flesh)
- 1 cup of milk
- ¼ cup of butter
- 1 pinch of salt

- To Serve:
- 1 tbsp of olive oil
- 1 sprig of parsley

DIRECTIONS

1. To prepare the mashed potatoes, start washing them, then put them in a pot full of water, bring them to a boil, and count about 30 minutes of cooking from the moment of boiling.
2. In truth, the exact cooking time may depend on both the size of the potatoes and the quality of the same, so you should always insert them with a fork to check that they are ready.
3. When cooked, drain and peel them while still hot.
4. Pass them through a potato masher and collect the puree directly in a pan.
5. Add the milk, the pieces of butter and a pinch of salt, and stir well over medium heat to mix the ingredients.
6. Your mashed potatoes are ready. Serve them hot, with a drizzle of olive oil and a little chopped fresh parsley.

The cabbage and carrot salad (coleslaw) is a side dish of Irish origin, trendy in all Anglo-Saxon countries. It is always on our Christmas table, one of my favorite side dishes.

INGREDIENTS

- 1.1 lbs of Cabbage 500 g
- 2/3 cup of Carrots
- 1Fresh spring onion
- for the dressing
- ½ cup of white yogurt
- 1 tbsp of White wine vinegar
- 1 tsp of Mustard
- 1 tbsp of Sugar
- 2 tbsp of Chopped chives
- 3 tbsp of Mayonnaise
- Salt to taste
- Black pepper to taste

DIRECTIONS

1. Let's prepare the Coleslaw! Peel the carrots and cut them into julienne strips (or you can buy carrots already cut into sticks).
2. Remove the outermost leaves of the cabbage and cut the rest into thin slices, thus obtaining a julienne.
3. Mix the carrots and the cabbage in a salad bowl and add the onion, very finely sliced.
4. Let's prepare the sauce! In a bowl, mix the yogurt with the mayonnaise, then add mustard, vinegar, sugar, salt, and pepper.
5. Finally, add the chives (keeping some to decorate the dish).
6. Taste and season with salt if necessary.
7. Dress the vegetable julienne with the dressing obtained.
8. Serve coleslaw immediately or keep it in the refrigerator.

43. CRUNCHY BACON AND POTATO SALAD

SERVES: 4   **PREP:** 15'   **COOKING:** 40'

This typical American everyday salad becomes a special guest at Christmas. As a child, I loved it, but I love it all today!

INGREDIENTS

- 4 cups of potato
- ½ cup of smoked bacon
- 5 tbsp of olive oil
- 1 tablespoon of White vinegar
- 1 tablespoon of mustard
- 1 tbsp of chives
- Salt and pepper

DIRECTIONS

1. Boil the potatoes. Peel them using the potato peeler and wash them.
2. Place them in a pot with plenty of lightly salted cold water and cook them for 30 minutes from boiling.
3. Drain them into a large bowl with a slotted spoon. Alternatively, wash them very well, scrub them with a brush, and cook them with the peel for 30-35 minutes. When they are still hot, peel them, and place them in the bowl.
4. Make the sauce.
5. While the potatoes are cooking, pour 4-5 tablespoons of extra virgin olive oil, 1 tablespoon of white vinegar into the jar. Add 1 tablespoon of old-fashioned mustard (grains) and a pinch of salt and pepper. Wash 15-20 chive stems and cut them with scissors, dropping them into the jar.
6. Close it with the lid and shake firmly. Sprinkle the potatoes with the sauce and mix.
7. Toast the bacon. Cut the slices of 100 g of bacon or smoked bacon into small pieces and heat the non-stick pan without adding fat. Combine the bacon pieces and let them fry so they are golden and crunchy, turning them at least once or shaking the pan.
8. Drain them on a kitchen paper towel, dab them with other paper and transfer them to the bowl with the potatoes. Mix and serve immediately.
9. Alternatively, brown the bacon slices whole in the non-stick pan 1-2 minutes per side. Drain them on a paper towel, cut them into small pieces, and mix them with the potato salad.
10. This delicious salad is ready to be served.

44. PUMPKIN FLAN

What we cook at Christmas is a light version of pumpkin flan. This is because, given the "heaviness" of the other recipes, a creamy side dish suits us perfectly!

INGREDIENTS

- 20 oz of pumpkin pulp
- 4 eggs
- 2 cups milk
- 1 tsp of dried oregano

- Olive oil to taste
- Salt and pepper to taste

DIRECTIONS

1. First, wash and dry the pumpkin pulp.
2. Cut it into cubes and steam for about 20 minutes.
3. Drain the pumpkin and let it cool.
4. Transfer the squash to a bowl.
5. Add salt, pepper, oregano, milk, and eggs to the bowl. Mix and then blend everything with an immersion blender.
6. Take a round pan and brush it with olive oil. Pour the pumpkin mixture inside.
7. Let cook in the preheated oven at 380°F [190°C] for 20 minutes.
8. Check the cooking and if the pumpkin flan is cooked, take it out of the oven; otherwise, continue cooking for another 5 minutes.
9. As soon as it is cooked, let it cool slightly and pour the contents onto a serving dish.
10. Cut the pumpkin flan into slices and serve.

SERVES: 5   PREP: 20'   COOKING: 25'

Who doesn't like sweet potatoes? This hummus can be the ideal alternative to the more classic mashed potatoes.

INGREDIENTS

- 4 cups of sweet potatoes
- 2 cups of cooked chickpeas
- 2 tbsp of tahini
- 1 tsp of chopped chili
- Olive oil to taste
- 1 tbsp of chopped parsley
- Salt to taste

DIRECTIONS

1. First, peel, wash and dry the sweet potatoes, rinse them under running water, and then cut it into cubes.
2. Put the sweet potato cube in a baking pan brushed with olive oil.
3. Season with oil, salt, and place in the oven.
4. Cook at 405°F [210°C] for 20-25 minutes.
5. Once they are cooked, remove the baking pan from the oven, and put the potatoes in a bowl.
6. Add the chickpeas, tahini, two tablespoons of oil and chili, and blend with an immersion blender until you get a smooth and homogeneous mixture.
7. Put the sweet potato hummus in a serving bowl, sprinkle with a bit of oil, chopped parsley, and serve.

DESSERTS

SERVES: 4   PREP: 30'   COOKING: 5h

Christmas Pudding is the quintessential Christmas cake of the British tradition, a rich and hearty delight that is prepared for the holidays.

INGREDIENTS

- 5 oz of sultanas
- 5 oz of Corinthian uvette
- 5 oz of cane sugar
- 1 cup of bread
- 1 cup of rum
- 2 tbsp of chopped almonds
- 4 tbsp dried figs (chopped)
- 4 tbsp of candied citron
- 4 tbsp dehydrated apricots (chopped)
- 1 tbsp of candied cherries
- 1/2 beer glass
- 5 oz of flour
- 5 oz g lard
- 4 eggs
- 1 tablespoon of molasses
- 1 lemon or orange
- 1 tsp of powdered cinnamon
- 1 tsp of nutmeg
- 20 ginger powder
- 1 tsp of Jamaican pepper
- Salt to taste

DIRECTIONS

1. Mix all the raisins, dried figs, apricots, cedar, and cherries in a bowl and sprinkle with 80 ml of rum and beer.
2. Add the grated zest and orange juice (lemon). Cover and let it rest for 12 hours.
3. Break the eggs into another large bowl. Beat them with the sugar; when they are well blended, add the cinnamon, a generous grating of nutmeg, grated ginger, and a grind of Jamaica pepper.
4. Add the molasses and the breadcrumbs.
5. Mix and pour the dried fruit mixture into this bowl. Add the chopped almonds and another 2 tbsp of rum (or cognac) to mix.
6. Finally, add the flour, lard, and a pinch of salt.
7. Grease a pudding mold, pour in the mixture, and level it.
8. Make a disc of parchment paper

with a diameter equal to the molds.

9. Grease it on one side and put it with the buttered side in contact with the dough.

10. Cover with another sheet of parchment paper that you will secure with several turns of kitchen twine.

11. Cover everything with an aluminum foil in which you will form two folds that will open with the formation of steam.

12. Pour plenty of hot water into a large pan to hold the mold to cover 1/3 of the mold.

13. Bake in a water bath at 375°F [190°C] for 4-6 hours.

14. Remove the cake and wait at least 48 hours before eating it.

SERVES: 8   PREP: 30'   COOKING: 55'

This recipe, similar to Halloween, is the most classic pie version. Her scent could be smelled right from my room, and I couldn't wait to get to dessert to eat her on Christmas.

INGREDIENTS

- 6 oz of flour
- 1 cup of cold butter
- 1 cup of powdered sugar
- 2 eggs
- For the cream:
- 1 cup of pumpkin pulp
- ½ of whipping cream
- 1 cup of sugar
- 1 tbsp of honey
- ½ tsp of cinnamon
- 1 tsp of powdered ginger
- 1 tsp of cloves

DIRECTIONS

1. Prepare pie dough. Place the flour and the butter cut into chunks in a bowl.
2. Start working with your hands until you get a sandy mixture.
3. Add the sugar and keep on kneading.
4. With the mixture, form a sort of fountain and place the egg inside. Knead until you get a lump-free and homogeneous mixture.
5. Form the mixture into a ball, cover it with cling film and refrigerate to rest for 30/40 minutes.
6. At the same time, prepare to fill. Wash and dry the pumpkin pulp, cut it into cubes, and then steam it for 15 minutes.
7. Once the pumpkin is cooked, put it in a bowl and blend it with an immersion blender.
8. Let it cool, and put the sugar and egg in another bowl. Mix with an electric mixer until you get a light and fluffy mixture.
9. Add the honey, cinnamon, cloves and ginger, and mix well. Add the pumpkin puree and mix until you get a homogeneous cream.
10. Put the whipping cream in a bowl and whisk it lightly until you get a

frothy mixture.

11. Add the whipping cream to the pumpkin cream and mix well.

12. Take the dough from the fridge and roll it out with a rolling pin until you get a thin sheet.

13. Brush a tart mold with olive oil and put the dough inside.

14. Fill the dough with the ginger pumpkin cream and then put the mold in the oven.

15. Cook at 340°F [170°C] for 50-55 minutes, then raise the temperature to 360°F [180°C] and cook for another 5 minutes.

16. Once cooked, remove the mold from the oven and let it cool. When it has cooled, remove it from the mold and place it in a serving dish.

17. Cut the cake into slices and serve.

SERVES: 4   **PREP:** 15'

A classic in the period from Thanksgiving to Christmas, there are many versions. I wanted to show you a much simpler one we used to make at home. As a child, I could not taste it due to the presence of brandy and rum. Now it cannot be missing as a dessert on my Christmas table.

INGREDIENTS

- 1.1 lbs of Milk
- 1 cup of whipping cream
- 1 glass of Brandy
- 1 glass of Rum

- 1 cup and 2 tbsp of Sugar
- 5 Eggs
- 1 tsp of ground cinnamon

DIRECTIONS

1. First, divide the yolks from the whites.
2. Whip the egg whites until stiff and set aside.
3. Put the egg yolks in a bowl together with the sugar and beat them with an electric whisk until the mixture is whitish and frothy.
4. Continuing to beat with whips, add the rum, brandy, cream and milk and beat for another 5 minutes.
5. Now add the whipped egg whites and mix them with the rest of the ingredients, mixing from bottom to top with a spatula, trying not to over-sell it.
6. Put the eggnog in glasses and sprinkle with ground cinnamon or a pinch of nutmeg.
7. You can serve your eggnog.

SERVES: 4   **PREP:** 1h   **COOKING:** 15'

Gingerbread is a very greedy dough with an intense and decisive aroma of spices; first, the ginger powder, followed by cinnamon, cloves, and nutmeg. A Christmas classic, I had a lot of fun forming men as a child.

INGREDIENTS

- 1 tsp of Ginger powder
- 12 oz of all-purpose flour
- 1 pinch ground cloves
- 1 pinch of Nutmeg
- 1 tsp of Cinnamon powder
- ¼ tsp of Bicarbonate
- 5 oz of Sugar
- ½ cup of Cold fridge butter
- 1 Egg
- 1 pinch of Salt
- 3 tbsp of Honey
- For the icing
- 1 cup and 2 tbsp of Powdered sugar
- 1 Egg white

DIRECTIONS

1. To make the gingerbread cookies, start with the spiced shortcrust pastry: pour the flour and all the spices into the mixer fitted with blades: ground cloves, ground cinnamon, grated nutmeg, and ginger powder. Also, add 1/4 teaspoon of baking soda and granulated sugar.

2. Then add a pinch of salt and pour in the honey.

3. Lastly, pour the cold butter from the fridge, cut it into cubes, and blend the mixture intermittently. Do not overheat the dough until you get a sandy consistency.

4. Pour the mixture on the work surface and form the classic fountain.

5. Pour the egg into the center and incorporate it into the dough first with the fork, then with your hands. Knead quickly and once the dough has taken on consistency, form a flat loaf and cover it with cling film.

6. Place the dough to harden in the refrigerator for at least 30 minutes.

7. After resting, resume the dough, and roll it out with a rolling pin on a floured pastry board to a thickness between 0,28 and 0,39

inches [1 cm].

8. Cut out the pastry with the Christmas molds you prefer, we have chosen the classic gingerbread men. Now pierce the cookies at the height of the little men's heads to pass a ribbon and hang them on the tree.

9. With the indicated doses, you will get about 15-16 cookies (depending on the type of shapes used and the size, the number may vary).

10. Transfer the cookies to a baking tray lined with baking paper. Bake the cookies in a static oven preheated to 395°F [200°C] for about 15 minutes. The times are indicative since each oven has a different power. Therefore, it is advisable to test it with a couple of pieces to ensure that the cooking in your oven is optimal.

11. When cooked, take the biscuits out of the oven, and let them cool completely, preferably on a wire rack.

12. Meanwhile, prepare the royal icing. Pour the egg whites into a bowl, and start whipping with the electric whisk at medium speed. Gradually incorporate the icing sugar with the help of a spoon: you will have to add until you obtain a homogeneous mixture of the desired consistency.

13. Transfer the icing into a disposable pastry bag and cut out the tip by creating a small hole, then decorate the biscuits by tracing the shape and enriching the men with details as you wish.

14. Now let's enjoy gingerbread cookies together!

SERVES: 4/6 **PREP:** 2h **COOKING:** 40'

Mince pies are delicious sweets typical of Anglo-Saxon Christmas. They are like tarts but slightly higher. These sweets, Santa's favorites, on the night of the coward, we leave him two or three cakes on the edge of the fireplace to thank him, along with a carrot for the reindeer.

INGREDIENTS

- For the Crust pie:
- 11.2 oz of flour
- 1 cup of butter
- 1 teaspoon of salt
- 1 tablespoon of sugar
- 1 glass of ice water
- For the stuffing:
- 1 apple
- 1/3 cup of brown sugar
- ½ cup of dried red fruits (blueberries, currants, and blackberries)
- ½ cup of sultanas
- 3 tbsp of dried apricots
- 3 tbsp of candied orange peel
- 1 tbsp of peeled almonds
- 1 teaspoon of cinnamon
- 1 teaspoon of ginger
- 1 pinch of nutmeg
- grated zest of 1 lemon
- ¼ cup of melted butter
- ½ cup of Brandy or Sherry or Rum

DIRECTIONS

1. First, prepare the filling. Finely chop the orange peel, the apricots, and the almonds. Place all the dried fruit in a bowl, along with the raisins, blueberries, and the grated lemon peel. Turn well.

2. Add the spices and sugar and the chopped apple. Turn everything together and add the fresh melted butter. Turn again, and then add the brandy.

3. Now all the pieces are separated, and the mixture is moist. Seal with cling film and leave to marinate for 1-2 days at room temperature, mixing every 6-7 hours.

4. If you want, you have time. You can leave the filling in the fridge and let it marinate for 1 or 2 weeks, always taking care to turn from time to time. After 2 days, the filling is very fragrant.

5. Prepare the Crust pie just before making your Mince Pies.

6. Arrange the flour, sugar, and salt in a bowl. Mix everything well

together. Add the cold butter into small pieces and mash with a fork as if to sandblast. Crumble well. Add iced water from the fridge.

7. Turn. In a few seconds, the mixture will compact into a soft dough. Form a ball. Place in the fridge for at least 1 hour.

8. Roll out the crust pie dough to a thickness of about 1.5 inches [4 cm]. Cut out circles with a pastry bowl approximately 4 inches in diameter [10 cm]. You can use the tart mold. Carving the foundation for the shell.

9. As you make the circles, place them in a previously greased and floured Muffin mold. Place the shells in the muffin tin. Place 2 - 3 tablespoons of filling in each shell, arriving a few millimeters from the edge.

10. Put the mold in the fridge with the shells. Always roll out the rest of the dough to a thickness of 1.5 inches [4 cm], and cut some stars, which must cover the surface of the mince pies, excluding the edges.

11. Take the pan out of the fridge and add the large star to the Mince pies, which cover the filling, then add the small one on top. Close the surface of the mince pie with star-shaped biscuits on the surface. Place the pan in the fridge for at least 30 minutes.

12. After this time, preheat the oven to 395ºF [200ºC]. Put the Mince pies in the oven and cook for about 30 - 40 minutes.

13. After the first 15-20 minutes, check the situation. Move the mince pies to the bottom of the oven for 10 minutes. Then bring them back to the central part.

14. Mince pies are ready when they are golden and not burnt. And the filling is perfectly compacted. Remove from the oven. Let it cool in the pan.

15. Take the mince pies out when they are lukewarm. A little bit of filling liquid could come out and flood the edges: it's normal, and it's nice that there are colored streaks. Use a long-pointed knife to remove the mince pies from the pan. Draw the contrast to detach any small pieces that have caramelized during cooking. They will come out perfect.

16. They are ready to be served when they are cold, so enjoyed or wrapped!